Soft Mutilations

Copyright © 2009 by Anne Hestand

ISBN 978-0-578-01550-7

36 fragments of an existence

(1992-2002)

By: anne hestand

Here are the fragments:

lost and furious

blinding and so incomplete

(acts)

1. It's time
2. Light
   ~~Somewhere in the~~
3. take
4. ~~the bleeder~~
5. the bleeder
6. Lottas
7/8 Somewhere in the dark / flip n' never etc
9. 9-5
10. ~~america~~
11. apart diet
12. Sad / ~~swallow~~
14. a~~t~~ guar
15/16 ~~layuya~~
17. ~~peso~~
18. I still came
19. ~~translation~~
20. a love song
21. ~~my left~~ Christian
22. I slpt mutilators
23. ~~a part diet~~ → the hayes
24. Pieces many parts
25. AWAke

My life

its time to exist
in between breath
in between shadow
while a mutilated generation
dictates where my fingers sleep.

Teeth

I have the world in the palm of my hand
but I can't get my tiny teeth around you.
When I shove my sex into the floorboards,
I break the children's teeth.
Please take me,
take me home
Wash my hair
and clean my German fingernails
forgive me for what I could not do.

starvation silence stillness

The Neighbors

Paying money to the man
for this
dirty dilation.
A noisy room
sticky with sex.
I live inside the people that hate me.
They hate America
and some days I understand.

keep it dirty

LIGHT

An unbearable light lives
in my neck
and when I move
this light stings my brain
with iridescent pictures.
 I record these lives
with 2 near dead
Hitler Blue Fingers.

a love story

please touch me
   in all the places
      i am raw
bruise me
   i don't mind
cause I need your breath
to steal the cancer
that turns these lines black

Exhaustion

Can't stick people together
Can't glue them to my spine
Can't forget my memory in this room
Maybe this is the reason why they nailed him to a stick
made glamorous incisions all over his body
And dripped invisible gods all over
our newborn skin.

Short and Viscous

I am a couple of teeth in a jar
Spoken in two tongues
I've been turned inside out
I am the wolf
in a war that does not feed.

1992

still lives, still breathing

still bleeding

i'm still bleeding in two

bitter pictures

that line the street

with a blatant disregard to all who came before

Take

I'll take home the most violent suicide.
The shortened phrases
           without hips.
The sticky remnants of paradise.
And the image of sense
           as they burst
the corrosive word out of your pituitary gland.
It's all part of a tiny somber existence
                held underwater in an exorcism.

Somewhere in the dark
The candle drowns
a martyr
His death sounds like cinnamon
I'm so hungry   wash all night

Soak yourself in blood milk
Your mouth has begun to fade
Singe my edges off
I want to be the roughest girl
My sourness drips more than the rest
It sliced you in 2
We re the same everyday,
all day
It still burns
I love this
I love you
Look at this   look at me.

Fractured

Today I am filled with fractures of light
that only exist in bright landscapes
where poets breathe with punctured lungs
and fingertips ache
with a fire that never goes out.

deux

It is only in between these lines that
            I exist.
A broken record.
A leaking shadow.
You could trace every bone.
There isn't a spot that could hide.
One eye sleeps and the other will follow.

I wish I could burn these frailties.
Tear my mediocrity to shreds.
Take the ghost out of this machine
   and put in a God instead.

1992

still lives, still breathing

still bleeding

i'm still bleeding

bitter pictures in two

they line the street

with a blatant disregard to all who came before

The Bleeder

I am animated by a body that dries in open spaces. I am bleeding faster than you.
I was open once but they complained of contamination.

It is my job to know when you're going to fall apart. To always say what you're afraid to. In silence, I live still. In the mourning, I starve.

Remember this, a writer mixes celestial ichor, confusion, and tears. An empty vessel full of language. Nothing else.

Come on over, and I'll rub these things into you backbone...

the future is here...
listerine hard

Absolution

Touch these belly verbs
and the sorry bitch ribs of verse
Everything I say turns into Christ
Language should be bound, gagged,
and slit down the middle
End of fucking story

Evolution

Sleeping all hours
Scratching insound
I will only
open my legs
to the most
violent words.
So they can
fuck me till I bleed
a whole new revolution.

Prenuptial Agreement

Still children preserved in formaldehyde
Still abortions dripping down my dress
Little girls praying on broken knees
Swallowing crushed gods at teatime
I am going to sell myself piece by piece
So when you come home there will be nothing left to fuck

Still Games

A fragment of a life
Spilled over concrete
Spread against the wall
His mouth is like water
It goes everywhere
The particles don't move
The flesh doesn't creep
And I try not to fracture my face
by moving the day.

The Art of Translation

The misplaced verb,
   the plural body.
Vicious noun, unfit preposition.
How I love your wicked, wicked ways.
MIS COM MUNI CATION
Rub your misuse in my face
Wash me in your filthy juice.
Punctuate me all night long
Leave me with your
filthy cum
dripping down
my american leg.

I enjoy falling apart
The dust from my skin
Fragments on the ground
Shredding the last kiss
This isn't the party we're supposed to attend
These word freaks clamoring for a vowel.
And I'm stuck in your shoe
A year to break glass
I love the sound of broken glass.
Chains created for the echo
There are too many people without eyes.
I wanted to be the one to
    discolor your cheeks
I wanted to be the pretty one.

9-5

I cannot believe in life
Twisting space
Always failing to shake
I cannot find a place to sit
So sick of my dirty hands
I hate to wash
I hate the white sky
I hate that at nine am we all line up to die.

Glass

I will lift this great portal of glass

without the loss of my sex.

She isn't protective of children

only the sad, secret creatures of Elysium

She comes clean by

dripping blood

all over the sad , sacred heads of Jesus Christ.

The Coldest War

I want to remember existence
And fight the silent revolution
that never ends clean
But poetry infects
all the neurons in my brain.
rendering me fucking useless
    My legs don't move.
    A cranial atrophy

Stuck to the floor
               I record all secrets...

Letters

Writing letters
to unknown Romanians
dying in the field.
I live abroad
and am beginning to starve.
The scars stitched.
neatly a millennium ago
are starting to give way
round my toes.
I am sorry
I write to you
I have no one else to speak to.

Moving House (WIP 2002)

Dragging my sores
From one trauma center
to anoyher trauma center
always
Re-packing the bags
Causw this shape has lomg expired
And my limB ARE bedgining to sweat sour milk
Momma I am ready to move
I am ready to go
bexause I can no longer hold these septic distortions inside

Soft Mutilations

I stand in the wall
of a corner I own.
In a room full
of naked asphyxiations
I create a womb
full of soft mutilations.
No more hard eyes
No more hard words
cutting into my hips.
I am far removed
from the things that
fight and starve.

Keep it real

Stood up

hide
in a corner
all seconds
hide
see if
you can
be still.
Nerves.
Pulses.
Tears
quiet the noise
sell your tar
settle your toes
go home
go home
lie still
 don't cry
go home.

Writing Pictures

I broke the radio in your back
for electrocuting me
in the middle of the night.
It fractured into tiny bright pieces
that stain my back
and burn my retina.
I write them down
so you won't forget
how easy I bruise
how quickly I move
when the pictures start to shake.

Goodnight

It's all the terrible sounds
        we make.
The dissatisfaction with movement
The hunger in my lungs
  and all the blood and vomit
  in my sink.
All I ever wanted out of this burst universe
    was a gentle suicide
      a smart end
      a sugared last taste.

LANGUAGE IS AWAKE.

It breathes. It fucks. It electrocutes. Feral and pulsing. A fetal sugar rape. Abusing and loving. It has the hottest blood. The strongest venom.

THIS IS OUR FUTURE.

The rules have gone. The bondage has been broken. Free and roaming. No more filling our teeth with the dehydrated syllables of long dead poets. No more antiquated rituals. Now is the time.

Language is HERE wide-eyed and ready for some fun.

Keep it violent

Anne Hestand was born in Georgia on April 18th 1977. She now lives in Liverpool England.

Acknowledgements

Thanks to daddy, momma, russ and t, duke, sammy, bama, the late great odessa, ellen, carol, charlie, the city of Liverpool, and brian holcombe for letting me use his artwork.

www.ingramcontent.com/pod-product-compliance
Lightning Source LLC
Chambersburg PA
CBHW020023050426
42450CB00005B/612